W9-BNJ-698

STECK-VAUGHN

PORTRAIT OF AMERICA

# North Carolina

**Steck-Vaughn Company**

| | |
|---|---|
| **Executive Editor** | Diane Sharpe |
| **Senior Editor** | Martin S. Saiewitz |
| **Design Manager** | Pamela Heaney |
| **Photo Editor** | Margie Foster |
| **Electronic Cover Graphics** | Alan Klemp |

**Proof Positive/Farrowlyne Associates, Inc.**
Program Editorial, Revision Development, Design, and Production

**Consultant:** North Carolina Department of Commerce, Travel & Tourism Division and the State Library, Division of Business and Industry

Published by Raintree Steck-Vaughn Publishers, an imprint of Steck-Vaughn Company.

A Turner Educational Services, Inc. book. Based on the Portrait of America television series by R. E. (Ted) Turner.

**Cover Photo:** Biltmore Estate by © Tom Algire/FPG International.

**Library of Congress Cataloging-in-Publication Data**

Thompson, Kathleen.
    North Carolina / Kathleen Thompson.
       p.  cm. — (Portrait of America)
    "Based on the Portrait of America television series" — T.p. verso.
    "A Turner book."
    Includes index.
    ISBN 0-8114-7378-3 (library binding). — ISBN 0-8114-7459-3 (softcover)
    1. North Carolina—Juvenile literature. [1. North Carolina.]
  I. Portrait of America (Television program) II. Title.
  III. Series: Thompson, Kathleen. Portrait of America.
  F254.3.T48 1996
  975.6—dc20                       95-26118
                                    CIP
                                    AC

Printed and Bound in the United States of America

2 3 4 5 6 7 8 9 10 WZ 03 02 01 00 99

**Acknowledgments**
The publishers wish to thank the following for permission to reproduce photographs:
P. 7 © Frederica Georgia/Photo Researchers; p. 8 Cherokee Historical Association; p. 10 North Carolina Travel & Tourism; p. 11 (top) North Carolina Division of Archives & History, (bottom) © Superstock; p. 12 North Carolina Travel & Tourism; p. 14 Orton Plantation; p. 15 Biltmore Estate; pp. 16, 17, 18 North Carolina Department of Cultural Resources, Division of Archives and History, Archives & Records Section; p. 19 UPI/Bettmann; p. 20 The Lost Colony; p. 21 Fort Raleigh National Historic Site; pp. 22, 23 The Lost Colony; p. 24 © Photri; p. 26 (top) Duke Homestead, (left) North Carolina Department of Cultural Resources, Division of Archives and History, Archives & Records Section; p. 27 (top) © Jim Knight/North Carolina Department of Agriculture, (bottom) Henredon Furniture, Inc.; p. 28 Henredon Furniture, Inc.; p. 29 (top left) North Carolina Travel & Tourism, (top right) Chimney Rock State Park, (bottom) Charlotte Convention & Visitors Bureau; p. 31 (both) Brooks Rogers, Inc.; p. 32 Biltmore Estate; p. 34 The North Carolina Symphony; p. 35 The Bettmann Archive; p. 36 UPI/Bettmann; p. 37 © Tim Barnwell/Folk Art Center; p. 38 The Charlotte Observer; p. 39 (both) Courtesy Art Centile; p. 40 © Martha Swope/Time, Inc.; p. 41 (both) North Carolina School of the Arts; p. 42 © Les Todd/Duke University Photo; p. 44 Research Triangle Foundation; p. 46 One Mile Up; p. 47 (left) One Mile Up, (center) North Carolina Travel & Tourism, (right) Illinois Tourism.

STECK-VAUGHN
PORTRAIT OF AMERICA

# North Carolina

Kathleen Thompson

A Turner Book

RSVP
RAINTREE
STECK-VAUGHN
PUBLISHERS
The Steck-Vaughn Company

*Austin, Texas*

**North Carolina**

WRIGHT BROTH
NATIONAL MEMO

Albemarle
Sound

**Kitty Hawk**

Roanoke River

GREAT SMOKY
MOUNTAINS

APPALACHIAN MOUNTAINS

**Greensboro**

**Winston-Salem**

**Durham**

**Chapel Hill**

**Rocky Mount**

Mount Mitchell

Yadkin River

☆

**RALEIGH**

Neuse River

Pamlico Sound

**Asheville**

BLUE RIDGE
MOUNTAINS

**Charlotte**

**Gastonia**

**Fayetteville**

**New Bern**

CAPE HATTERAS
NATIONAL SEASHORE

**Wilmington**

# Contents

# Introduction

The boundaries of North Carolina enclose some of the best land in the United States. The eastern coast is marked by wetlands—lagoons and marshes that separate the mainland from a chain of barrier islands called the Outer Banks. These wetlands provide a home for a variety of birds and other species of wildlife. The rolling hills in the center of the state are home to industrial cities as well as farmland. Western North Carolina has towering, forest-covered mountain ranges.

Throughout history, North Carolina's people also have represented the best characteristics of the United States. From the founding of the colonies to the present day, the actions of North Carolinians have been followed and their voices heard. North Carolina encompasses America's beauty, struggles, and strengths all in a single state.

Grandfather Mountain, in the Blue Ridge Mountains, is well named. Its rounded contours are the result of millions of years of weathering and erosion.

# North Carolina

# Generations of Progress

Five hundred years ago, the area we now call North Carolina was home to about 35,000 Native American people. Among the largest of these groups were the Cherokee, Hattera, Catawba, Chowanoc, and Tuscarora. These groups and others spread throughout forty thousand square miles, covering nearly all the territory of present-day North Carolina. They farmed the land and lived in towns. They made their own clothes and blankets as well as tools, utensils, and pottery.

In 1524, Giovanni da Verrazano became the first European to explore the coast of North Carolina. About two years later, Spanish explorer Lucas Vásquez de Ayllón attempted to organize a colony near Cape Fear. The settlers were nearly wiped out by sickness and starvation, however. In 1540 Spanish explorer Hernando de Soto visited present-day North Carolina in his search for gold. When he found none, he moved on. During the next 45 years, Spanish and French explorers traveled throughout this land, but none of them stayed.

Basketmaking among Native American groups dates as far back as prehistoric times. Basketmaking techniques that developed over the years are still used by Native Americans today.

This is a replica of a late 1500s sailing ship. Sir Walter Raleigh's colonists crossed the Atlantic to present-day North Carolina on ships like this one.

In 1587 Sir Walter Raleigh provided money for a group of English settlers to establish a colony on Roanoke Island. John White, the leader of the colony, went to England later in the year to obtain supplies. When he returned to Roanoke in 1590, White found that his colony had vanished without a trace. To this day, no one knows what happened.

In 1629 King Charles I awarded Sir Robert Heath the area south of Virginia almost to Florida. The new territory, which Heath named "Carolana" after King Charles, included present-day North Carolina, South Carolina, and part of Georgia.

In the mid-1600s, people from Virginia journeyed south to Carolina. They settled in the area around what is now Albemarle Sound. These Virginians came on their own and lived under their own laws until 1663. In that year King Charles II took the Carolina charter away from Heath and gave it to eight of his close friends. They were known as the Lords Proprietors, which means they were ruling landowners. The Lords Proprietors ruled from England. They appointed governors to rule the colony, which was split into three counties: Albemarle, Clarendon, and Craven.

The colonists had tasted self-rule, however, and did not want to be governed from a foreign land. They especially did not want to be governed by men who saw Carolina as a business run for profit. In 1677 a group of colonists in Albemarle seized their governor and threw him in jail. Then they elected an assembly, collected taxes, and governed the colony themselves. They also elected their own governor, a land surveyor named John Culpeper. The uprising came to be called the Culpeper Rebellion.

The Lords Proprietors sent another governor to rule Albemarle, however. By 1688 the colonists put the governor on trial, and he was removed from office. It wasn't until 1691 that the people of Carolina accepted a governor from England. This governor was appointed for the whole region, not just one of the three counties. In 1712 the colony of Carolina was divided into North Carolina and South Carolina, and a deputy governor was placed in charge of each.

In the years between 1650 and 1712, more settlers came into North Carolina. They settled on large areas of land that had formerly been used only by Native Americans. The settlers cut down trees to clear the land for farming. This destroyed the forest home of the deer and other animals the Native Americans hunted.

Charles II became king of England in 1660. He acted quickly to bring the colonies more tightly under control.

Cape Lookout is at the southern end of the Outer Banks, a series of offshore islands that stretch along much of North Carolina's Atlantic coast.

In Old Salem restored buildings and costumed actors show what colonial life was like.

Finally, the Tuscarora decided they had to take action. In 1711 they attacked New Bern and other settlements along the Neuse and Pamlico rivers. The Tuscarora killed most of the settlers, burning their homes and destroying their crops. The Tuscarora War raged for a year and a half until the Native Americans were defeated.

During the early 1700s, coastal towns suffered from the raids of marauding pirates. The most feared of these was Edward Teach, known as "Blackbeard." In 1718 Blackbeard was killed in a battle near Ocracoke Island.

In 1729 the Lords Proprietors sold the colony to King George II, making North Carolina a royal colony. Settlers from Great Britain and other colonies flooded into the area. Most of the new residents came from Pennsylvania, Virginia, and South Carolina. North Carolina's population increased from about 35,000 in 1730 to 350,000 in 1775.

The years of colonization in America were marked by almost constant wars. The British and French claimed much of the same land, so they fought each other. The French and the English also fought the Spanish, who claimed much of the southern part of North America. The settlers fought groups of Native Americans. Some Native American groups sided with the British, but most were allied with the French. During the French and Indian War, fought between 1754 and 1763, the British and their Native American llies fought the French and their Native American llies. The British forced the French to give up their claims in North America.

After the French and Indian War, Great Britain tried to make up its war expenses by placing heavy taxes on the colonists. North Carolina was in the forefront of the rebellion against these taxes. North Carolina citizens formed groups called the Sons of Liberty and the Regulators. These groups organized protests and took part in skirmishes with British troops. In Edenton in 1774, a group of women gathered to pledge their support for independence. The event was one of the first examples of organized political activity by women in the colonies. It was known as the Edenton Tea Party.

When the Revolutionary War began in 1775, North Carolina colonists split into opposing camps. Groups against the revolution thought the colonies would be better off being owned by Great Britain. These people were called Tories or Loyalists. Those people who wanted independence were known as Whigs or patriots. In February 1776, armed Whigs and Tories fought each other near Wilmington. The Whigs won an overwhelming victory. Later that year, when the Continental Congress met and drafted the Declaration of Independence, North Carolina was the first colony to tell its delegates to vote in favor of independence. Also in 1776 North Carolina approved its first constitution.

An important battle of the Revolutionary War was fought in North Carolina, and it was crucial to the war's outcome. British general Charles Cornwallis fought his way north through South Carolina in 1780. He lost badly in the battles of Cowpens and Kings Mountain near the north-central border of South Carolina. On March 15, 1781, Cornwallis's troops met the Americans in battle at Guilford Courthouse in central North Carolina. Although Cornwallis's army won that battle, they were severely weakened by the effort. Seven months later General Cornwallis surrendered his army of six thousand men at Yorktown, Virginia.

In 1787, representatives from the 13 former colonies gathered in Philadelphia, Pennsylvania, to create a new government. There were serious disagreements about how strong the central government should be. The people of North Carolina were concerned about the rights of the individual states. They refused to approve the Constitution until certain amendments were added that would protect citizens from govern-

The main house at Orton Plantation in Wilmington is an excellent example of pre-Civil War architecture. Although North Carolina did not have as many large plantations as some Southern states, its plantation owners were very rich and powerful.

ment abuse. The supporters of the Constitution promised these changes would be made and North Carolina signed the Constitution in 1789. In December 1791, ten amendments called the Bill of Rights were added to the Constitution.

During the early 1800s, North Carolina had many small farms and a few large plantations. Tobacco and cotton were the major crops. The invention of the cotton gin in 1793 improved North Carolina's economy greatly. This machine separated the cotton fibers from the seeds quicker than human hands could. Cotton production grew but North Carolina's dependence on only two crops eventually created problems. Growing these same crops year after year used up the nutrients in the soil. Farmers abandoned worn-out fields, which were further destroyed when the topsoil washed away in the rains. In addition, there were a number of bad years for crops. Many farmers just packed up and moved away. About half the countries in the state lost population in the 1830s.

North Carolina revised its constitution in 1835 to give more political power to people in the western part of the state. Political power was more evenly distributed among taxpayers instead of being controlled only by wealthy owners of large plantations. The state legislature also encouraged the development of new farmlands in the western part of the state.

This dining room is one of the 250 rooms in the main house at Biltmore, in Asheville. The house was built in the 1800s by the wealthy Vanderbilt family.

By the 1840s slavery and the rights of states were major issues in the United States. Northern states generally favored a strong federal government and were against slavery. Most Southern states wanted more state power, and they were determined to keep slavery. The South's economy was almost entirely dependent on agriculture, and slaves were the cheapest form of manual labor. Although North Carolina permitted slavery, it was not one of the major slave-owning states. However, in 1860 about one-third of North Carolina's population were slaves. There were about 35,000 slave-owning families in the state at that time.

The Civil War brought a difficult decision for North Carolina. North Carolina favored slavery, but it was also one of the 13 original colonies. Its people believed in states' rights, but they did not want to leave the Union. In the early months of 1861 seven states—all of them from the South—formed the Confederate States of America. A month later President Abraham Lincoln asked North Carolina for troops to fight against the Confederacy. North Carolinians were not willing to do this, so the state left the Union, too. It was the last southern state to do so.

During the Civil War, some units of the 69th Infantry of the Confederate Army were composed of Cherokee soldiers.

North Carolina lost more men in the war than any other Southern state. One fourth of all the soldiers who died fighting for the Confederacy were from North Carolina.

The period following the Civil War was called Reconstruction. During this time the federal government tried to help former slaves take part in a free society. Former slaves were given voting rights, and some joined the Republican party, the party of Abraham Lincoln, and were elected as governors and Congressmen. In 1868 North Carolina was governed by the Republicans. However, some citizens were opposed to African Americans having these rights. Terrorist organizations such as the Ku Klux Klan sprang up all over the South. These organizations worked to reverse many of the freedoms African Americans had only recently gained. By 1870 the Republican party had lost its control in North Carolina and in most of the rest of the South.

North Carolina's economy recovered slowly from the Civil War. Except that the former slaves were free, not much had changed. North Carolina was still primarily a farming state. Tobacco and cotton were still the major sources of income, but without slaves to work the fields, production sagged. It wasn't until the 1880s that farm production reached pre-Civil War levels.

After the Civil War, many former slaves became sharecroppers. They worked on land owned by a planter in return for a share of the harvest.

Orville and Wilbur Wright flew the first motorized airplane at Kitty Hawk on December 17, 1903. The plane reached a top speed of thirty miles per hour.

By the end of the nineteenth century, North Carolina began manufacturing products made from its crops. Tobacco processing became an important industry. Lumber, furniture, and cotton textiles broadened the state's economy. By the late 1920s, North Carolina led the country in all three of these industries. But North Carolina, like the rest of the country, suffered greatly from the Great Depression of the 1930s.

During the Depression industries and banks across the country closed. Millions of people were out of work. In North Carolina many farmers lost their land because markets could not afford to buy their crops. The economies of North Carolina and the nation recuperated when the United States entered World War II in 1941. The federal government needed manufactured goods for the war effort, and the demand for North Carolina's products was renewed.

In 1954 the United States Supreme Court ruled that segregation in public schools was unconstitutional. Segregation is the practice of separating people, usually by color or ethnic heritage. North Carolina fought the ruling. The state voted to pay private school tuition for any child "assigned to a public school attended by a child of another race." School districts could simply close their schools rather than admit African Americans. North Carolina voters passed these laws, but they were later declared unconstitutional by the courts.

African Americans battled segregation in public places by staging protests known as "lunch counter demonstrations." The first of these demonstrations was held in Greensboro in 1960. African Americans protested by going to segregated restaurants. Although they suffered threats and taunts, the protesters usually stayed until they were arrested. Protests such as these made a public display of the injustice of segregation. Later, this tactic was used in many other southern towns. The attention these demonstrations gained spurred Congress to pass the Civil Rights Act of 1964. By the early 1970s, most of the public schools in North Carolina had been officially desegregated.

In the 1970s large numbers of people left North Carolina for better economic opportunities in northern cities. This trend reversed in the 1980s, however. One reason may have been the state's open spaces and high-tech capabilities. North Carolina has worked to support the development of new technologies. This and reduced corporate taxes have brought many high-tech businesses into the state.

North Carolina was once thought of as a sleepy place. Today, North Carolina is booming. The 1990 federal census showed it is one of the top ten most-populated states. The state's government has placed increased emphasis on education, the arts, and quality of life. There is no doubt that North Carolina is wide awake and looking toward a bright future.

African American students protest the segregation of a lunch counter in Greensboro with a sit-in demonstration.

# The Lost Colony

Before the Pilgrims established Plymouth in 1620, and before English settlers founded Jamestown in 1607, there was another English colony—Roanoke. Roanoke Island lies off the coast of North Carolina, near Albermarle Sound. Much is known about the Jamestown and Plymouth colonies. People today can trace their family roots to these settlements. But what of the Roanoke colony? Are there any descendants of these colonists? No one knows for sure. The Roanoke colony vanished without a visible trace, and the mystery has remained unsolved for more than four hundred years.

English explorers first landed at the Outer Banks of North Carolina in the summer of 1584. The sailors were excited to discover these islands. It was spring, the weather was wonderful, and the Native American groups were friendly and helpful. One Native American, a Croatoan by the name of Wanchese, took the explorers to visit a small island nearby. Roanoke Island was six miles wide and twelve miles long. The explorers decided the island was a good place to settle. They stayed about five weeks, trading with the friendly

*This is a scene from the outdoor play, "The Lost Colony." The play is produced at Fort Raleigh every summer.*

Croatoan and learning how to grow maize (corn) and other crops.

When the explorers returned to England, they gave a glowing report of Roanoke Island. Soon a group of people was assembled to go to Roanoke and build homes for others who would follow. The expedition was led by Sir Richard Grenville. Seven ships set off from England on April 9, 1585. Bad luck befell them before they even reached the island. The colonists lost their supplies in a storm. After they reached the island, some people immediately returned to England for more supplies.

During their stay on the island, Grenville's silver drinking cup was reported missing, and he blamed the Native Americans for stealing it. When the cup did not turn up, Grenville and some soldiers burned a village of a neighboring Native American group, the Secotan.

Nearly a year passed without the arrival of supplies from England. The colonists were discouraged and fearful of revenge from the Native Americans. Many of them joined the occupants of another English ship that came by. Fifteen men stayed behind to care for the small settlement.

21

In 1587 a second group of colonists set sail from England for the Chesapeake Bay area. Their leader, John White, and his navigator, Simon Fernando, planned to take the remaining colonists on Roanoke Island to the new Chesapeake colony. When they reached the island, Fernando refused to take White and the colonists on to Chesapeake. Fernando wanted to return to England before the winter set in. White and the colonists would have to stay on hostile Roanoke Island for the winter. When White and the others examined the settlement, they discovered that all of the 15 who had remained on the island had been killed.

The colonists decided that John White should return to England with Fernando. When White returned in the spring with fresh supplies, they would move to the Chesapeake colony.

John White's arrival in England was met by bad news. England and Spain were planning to go to war, and all the available ships were being used to fight the Spanish. Finally, three years later, White made arrangements with a merchant who was about to set off for the West Indies. The merchant would carry White and the supplies to Roanoke before going his own way.

When White reached the colony on Roanoke Island, he did not find the colonists he had left behind. Nor did he discover any evidence of them. The

Colonists from England arrive at Roanoke Island in this scene from "The Lost Colony."

only clue that they were ever there was the word *Croatoan,* which had been carved into a wooden post. A search of the island showed that nothing else remained. The village and all the houses were gone. The overgrowth was evidence that nothing had been planted for many seasons. There were no skeletons and no signs of battle. An oncoming storm kept White and the merchant from searching any longer. The merchant had to leave for the West Indies. He promised John White that he would bring him back in the spring.

White and the merchant never reached the West Indies. The storm blew them far off course, so that they had to return to England. Over the years, other expeditions set out to discover what happened to the colonists on Roanoke Island. Each time, the searchers came back with different tales and probable explanations. None brought back evidence of survivors.

What could have happened to the colony? Some believe that they were on their way to stay with the Croatoan on another island, and that something must have happened on the way. Possibly the Spanish captured them, since the two countries were at war. But why was the village gone? Roanoke Island has provided no answers.

*A very young actress plays the part of Virginia Dare, the first English baby born in North America. Virginia Dare was born August 18, 1587. She disappeared along with all of the other colonists.*

# An Economic Success Story

North Carolina is a thriving industrial and agricultural state. Nearly one third of North Carolina's workforce is involved in manufacturing. This percentage is one of the highest in the nation. The three industries that have dominated the state for the last one hundred years are still vitally important. With fewer people smoking cigarettes, textiles have passed tobacco products as the state's most important product. North Carolina's textile mills produce more cloth than those in any other state. Whether it's yarn, hosiery, denim, or carpeting, North Carolina is a leader. Its mills also produce a wide variety of synthetic fabrics, as well as such household textiles as material for sheets and towels. The state also has hundreds of clothing factories.

Tobacco is North Carolina's second most important manufactured product. The state is responsible for manufacturing about half the cigarettes that are made in the United States. Recently, as more Americans have stopped smoking, North Carolina tobacco

North Carolina harvests more tobacco than any other state.

The Duke Homestead in Durham now is a historical site with a museum showing the history of tobacco and an early tobacco factory.

Around the turn of the century, James B. Duke's American Tobacco Company owned about 150 tobacco factories.

companies have stepped up their advertising and sales efforts in other nations.

During the 1970s chemical manufacturing moved into third place among North Carolina's industries. This was partly due to the huge increase in synthetic fibers demanded by the state's textile mills. Pharmaceuticals are the other major chemical products made in chemical manufacturing.

Other leading North Carolina products are electrical equipment, machinery, food products, and furniture. Even though furniture has slipped from third to sixth in value, North Carolina still produces more household furniture than any other state. Every year, thousands of furniture buyers from retail stores in over 100 countries come to High Point to see and order the latest furniture lines. So many factories are located in

High Point that it is known as the "Furniture Capital of the World."

At the same time, agriculture in North Carolina remains strong. The state has about sixty thousand farms that cover one-third of its land. Farm production is almost evenly divided between crops and livestock. Tobacco is the largest cash crop, providing about one fifth of the state's farm income. Among other crops, corn ranks second and soybeans third. Cotton is still grown, primarily in the southern and eastern parts of the state. Peanuts are a very important crop, as are cotton, wheat, and sweet potatoes.

Broiler chickens, those from five to twelve weeks old, are North Carolina's most important livestock farm product. Hogs rank second. The state is among the leading producers of both broilers and hogs. It is number one in the country in raising turkeys, which are its third-ranked livestock farm product. Farmers in the state also produce dairy cattle, beef cattle, eggs, and ducks. Also, fishers along the Atlantic Coast catch flounder, croaker, and sea trout. Coastal waters also produce shellfish, particularly crabs, oysters, shrimp, and clams.

Even though much tobacco picking is now done by machines, humans still have to check the progress of the crop as it grows toward maturity.

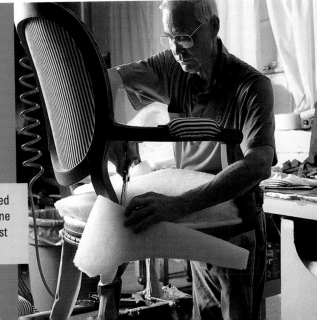

Making fine, hand-crafted household furniture is one of North Carolina's oldest industries.

Furniture buyers come from around the world to North Carolina showrooms such as this one to select the styles and pieces they will sell in their stores.

Service industries make up the largest sector of North Carolina's economy. These businesses provide services rather than making a product. In North Carolina, service industries account for about sixty percent of the state's economy. The largest single category of service industries is wholesale and retail trade. Retail businesses sell products to customers, and wholesale businesses supply the retail businesses with the products to sell. Selling textiles, clothing, tobacco products, and furniture is a large part of wholesale and retail trade.

Other important service industries are finance, insurance, real estate, and such personal services as doctors, lawyers, and repair shops. Another growing part of the service sector is made up of businesses that cater to North Carolina's thriving tourist industry. Tourism is another large sector of North Carolina's service industries.

Can North Carolina preserve its beauty and natural resources and still emphasize industrial growth? The chances are very good because North Carolinians care about preserving their environment. A survey of one hundred thousand residents showed that they rank conservation just as important as jobs and a healthy economy. This balance of concerns should keep North Carolina not only prosperous, but clean and lovely for generations to come.

*left.* North Carolina has many small farms. Here, a crop of pumpkins awaits sale at a roadside stand.

*right.* In western North Carolina, several mountain ranges provide spectacular scenery. These sightseers are ascending Chimney Rock, in the Blue Ridge Mountains.

Because it is an industrial and commercial hub, Charlotte is a symbol for the new South. Charlotte shows the South's transition from an agricultural economy to an industrial economy.

# Beauty in the Wood

Making furniture is big business in North Carolina. Dozens of major furniture manufacturers have their offices and factories there. In High Point, in north-central North Carolina, furniture-making is even more than big business. It's just about the only business.

Randy Culler was born in High Point. For him, becoming part of the furniture industry was as natural as breathing. "My grandfather had worked as a laborer in furniture factories as a young man. Then he started his own furniture-making business just before the Depression. He did well. By the time he died in 1956, he'd built three companies. My father had worked with him and took over when grandfather died."

Randy Culler could have become head of a manufacturing company, but he was more interested in design, the first step in the furniture-making process. A designer thinks up an idea for a piece of furniture, then makes sketches of the way it will look. Finally, the designer figures out how to manufacture the creation efficiently and makes technical drawings that illustrate this plan.

To learn the art of furniture design, Culler went to the Kendall College of Art and Design in Grand Rapids, Michigan. Kendall is one of the oldest and best design schools in the country. After graduation Culler worked for several years in Michigan.

He moved back to High Point and started his own design firm, RCR Development Corporation, in 1976. Today, his company designs for about a dozen regular clients throughout the United States, Mexico, Canada, and Europe. He enjoys designing modern furniture the most but says with a laugh, "In this business, you design whatever the retail trade demands. Recently, that's been traditional designs."

Once the sketches and technical drawings are done, RCR does something more. As far as Culler knows, his firm is the only design house in the country that actually builds the furniture it designs. Most designers just make the sketches and the technical drawings.

"We have six people, including me. My secretary also is a computer drafting expert, so she creates technical drawings. We have framers, who do woodworking, upholsterers, and pattern makers."

Together, they take wood and cloth and give life to Culler's ideas. The beauty he creates in his mind becomes beauty that people can see and touch. It's work Randy Culler loves, and that's what really counts.

*Randy Culler is shown here at his drafting table with a few of his designs behind him.*

*Randy Culler designs furniture that is comfortable, yet has a modern style.*

# A State of the Arts

One of the things in which the people of North Carolina can take great pride is their support of the arts. During the state's long history, its people have given time and money to establish libraries, museums, and musical and theatrical companies. The citizens are also dedicated to preserving the state's rich heritage.

North Carolina was the first state to support a symphony orchestra. It also claims the first state-supported school for the performing arts. This school, the North Carolina School of the Arts, is considered one of the best schools of its kind in the world. The North Carolina Arts Council helps support the North Carolina Dance Theater. The oldest continuously active brass band in the United States can be heard in Old Salem. The band has been around since 1769—with a few changes in membership, of course. The North Carolina Arts Council has done much work in teaching young artists and showing their work. The University of North Carolina, founded in 1795, is the oldest state university in the United States.

The Biltmore estate is a national historic landmark, covering 12,000 acres. It is the largest privately owned home in the United States and a popular tourist attraction.

Not all of North Carolina's long-standing arts are supported by the state. Cities participate as well. Greensboro, Charlotte, and Winston-Salem all have excellent symphony orchestras. In addition, Raleigh, Greensboro, and Charlotte have opera companies. In 1949, Winston-Salem became the first city in the United States to form an arts council, a group of people dedicated to supporting the arts in all ways. Since then the arts council movement has spread across the continent. More than four thousand cities in the United States and Canada now have arts councils. The Winston-Salem Arts Council helped form the American Council of the Arts, which is now called Americans for the Arts.

One of the greatest boosts to North Carolina's art scene took place in 1947. The state legislature voted to spend one million dollars to create a state-supported

The excellent North Carolina Symphony Orchestra is funded by contributions from hundreds of businesses throughout the state.

art museum. It took nine years to complete, but the North Carolina Museum of Art finally opened in 1956. Today, the museum, located in Raleigh, is considered one of the finest art museums in the South. Other fine art museums include the Weatherspoon Art Gallery in Greensboro and the Ackland Art Museum, part of the University of North Carolina at Chapel Hill.

Great individual writers and artists have grown up in North Carolina. One of the most famous was the novelist Thomas Wolfe. He was born in Asheville, North Carolina. His books include *Of Time and the River*, *You Can't Go Home Again*, and *Look Homeward, Angel*. In these novels Thomas Wolfe described life in small-town North Carolina and the kind of people he

Novelist Thomas Wolfe died when he was only 37 years old. But during his short life he wrote plays, many short stories, and four novels.

knew there. Wolfe's early interest in expression was greatly encouraged by the Carolina Playmakers. This drama workshop was founded in 1918 at the University of North Carolina.

Another participant in the Carolina Playmakers was Paul Green, whose play *In Abraham's Bosom* won the Pulitzer Prize in 1927. Green is also known as the "Father of Outdoor Drama." He wrote several historical plays intended to be performed outdoors in the settings where the plays occur. The best known of these is *The Lost Colony*, which has played on Roanoke Island every summer since 1937. These outdoor historical dramas are favorites in North Carolina. Other long-running plays include Kermit Hunter's *Unto These Hills*, about the destruction of the Cherokee nation, and a Daniel Boone biography called *Horn in the West* also by Hunter. *The Sword of Peace* by William Harcy dramatizes the dilemma faced by a peaceful but patriotic Quaker community during the Revolutionary War.

William Sydney Porter was one of the nation's most popular short-story writers during the last half of the nineteenth century. Porter wrote using the pen name O. Henry. Part of his popularity was due to his use of surprise endings. In 1943 Betty Smith from Chapel Hill finished her novel *A Tree Grows in Brooklyn*, a story about a North Carolina family trying to live in New York City. Probably North Carolina's best-selling writer today is Anne Tyler. Two of her most popular books are *Dinner at the Homesick Restaurant* and *The Accidental Tourist*. Tyler won a Pulitzer Prize in 1989 for her novel *Breathing Lessons*.

North Carolina's musical taste spans symphonies and opera to bluegrass, country, and gospel. Legendary jazz saxophonist John Coltrane came from Hamlet, North Carolina. Two of the state's most famous contemporary performers are bluegrass musician Earl Scruggs and soul singer Roberta Flack.

No description of the arts in North Carolina would be complete without mention of the folk arts. Generations of rural North Carolinians have woven their own cloth, built furniture, and stitched clothes and quilts. Many products of these folk arts are not seen in displays and are not for sale. They belong to the families in which they were handed down—the result of generations of skill, technique, and love.

North Carolina has played a role in influencing artists and supporting arts organizations. This commitment to culture is a commitment to its people. Support of the arts communicates the public message that self-expression is important.

At the Folk Art Center, near Asheville in western North Carolina, visitors can see the rich tradition of arts and crafts practiced by rural people from the earliest colonial days.

# Urban Pioneers

Jim and Eileen Hester are the kind of people some call urban pioneers. More than twenty years ago, they bought a boarded-up old house in a run-down section of Charlotte, North Carolina's largest city. At the time Eileen didn't see herself and her husband as pioneers. "People started calling us urban pioneers when we bought the house," she recalls. "At the time, I didn't think we were doing anything so unusual."

The house that Eileen and Jim bought was built in 1884. At that time, Charlotte was separated into four political divisions, called wards. The northwest quarter of the city was designated as the Fourth Ward. It contained many large and elegant homes where wealthy families had lived. Even the mayor of Charlotte lived in a Fourth Ward mansion.

In the 1930s the wealthy left the city for the suburbs, and the Fourth Ward entered a long period of decline. Many homes stood abandoned for years. Some were demolished or burned down. The house Jim and Eileen eventu-

When Eileen and Jim Hester first bought their house, it was in very bad shape. Fortunately its basic structure was sound, which allowed them to restore it.

ally bought was converted into four apartments in 1942. Then, in the early 1970s, the owner decided he couldn't afford the upkeep. So he boarded it up.

In 1975 a civic group called the Junior League of Charlotte got the idea that the Fourth Ward could be revived. The League purchased the house for $40,000, then spent $12,000 cleaning, painting, and refinishing it. Eileen and Jim Hester could finish fixing it up if they did the work themselves. The Hesters bought the house in 1976.

"The neighborhood was poor, but we felt there was enough community interest to make a redevelopment

the community must be willing to stay and help the area to grow.

Today, the Fourth Ward is once again a beautiful community. Many old homes have been restored. New homes have been built, too. "Even when we first moved in, we felt that this was a real neighborhood," said Eileen. "People would loan you tools or help you do something that needed an extra hand.

"People sit on their porches in the evening. You see folks out with their children or walking their dogs. You know your neighbors. That's a nice feeling."

project work," Jim said. "We felt very good about the Fourth Ward and what it could turn into."

Community interest is important to today's urban pioneers. People in

_Jim and Eileen work in the yard of the house they rehabilitated._

# Excellence on Stage

Mel Tomlinson has been a star of the New York City Ballet. He has danced in Boston and taught at Harvard University and the Boston Conservatory of Music. But his roots have remained in North Carolina, where he taught ballet at the Charlotte campus of the University of North Carolina.

Tomlinson is a product of the North Carolina School of the Arts. Founded in 1963 this was the first state-supported school of performing arts in the United States. Today, it is the only school in the world that provides professional training in the performing arts from the middle grades through graduate school. It offers programs in dance, drama, music, filmmaking, stage design, and production.

Approximately a thousand students are selected by audition. An audition is a trial performance on which the artist's talent is judged. Then, the students are placed in classes based on their ability, not on their age. The students represent more than forty states and twenty countries. Besides the arts, they study the academic subjects—English, math, history, language, and science.

The philosophy of the school is that talent is not enough to succeed in the performing arts. To make it as a professional performer, you need professional training. That means being taught by people like Mel Tomlinson who have won success on-stage, on-screen, and in concert halls. For years, Tomlinson came back to the School of the Arts during

*Ballet star Mel Tomlinson got his training at the North Carolina School of the Arts.*

*The Performance Place is the performing arts facility at the North Carolina School of the Arts.*

summers and off-seasons to each and inspire.

"It was exciting," said lina Gilreath Lucas, recalling Mel Tomlinson as a teacher. He was a role model. He was somebody the students could look up to." After graduating from the School of the Arts in the mid-1980s, Gilreath danced with the Dance Theatre of Harlem in New York City and with the Atlanta Ballet. In 1990 she and her husband began Ballethnic, an Atlanta-based, African American ballet company.

Gilreath still remembers her days at the School of the Arts. "Sometimes I got very discouraged. It seemed that no matter how hard I tried, things never worked out right. That's when discipline comes in. You do what you're supposed to do, then go to bed tired and sore, and get up and do it again the next day.

"But when I danced, and just enjoyed it, I felt very good. Now, when I teach my own students, I feel like I'm passing on something very precious that Mel and my other teachers passed along to me."

*Students perform in a drama workshop at the North Carolina School of the Arts.*

41

# Training for the Future

Like much of the South, North Carolina's economy was once based almost entirely on agriculture. Today, the state has a healthy economy based on a variety of industries. Compared to the rest of the country, North Carolina has a low rate of unemployment and a high level of literacy. But that doesn't mean it is not looking for ways to improve. North Carolina is preparing for the future with the best tool money can buy: education.

More and more jobs in the state—and in the country—are being lost to machines that can do the work of more than one worker. Future employers will need people with higher skills and a higher degree of education. It is in North Carolina's best interests to help its people acquire these skills, because skilled workers attract high-tech companies. Companies want to come to states where the people are trained.

Right now no one in North Carolina lives far from a college or technical institution. The universities in North Carolina are working with industries to provide

These students at Duke University in North Carolina are preparing themselves for future careers in high-tech businesses.

Research Triangle Park, in the Raleigh-Durham area, is a center for research in electronics and medicine.

the specific training that companies need. In addition, the Joint Partnership Retraining Act provides state funds to retrain workers whose jobs have already been lost to machines. The act also provides funds to find out what skills will be needed in the future.

These efforts are working. Many new high-tech industries have come to North Carolina. More are arriving every year. Many of these companies are from foreign countries. Very few states have as much foreign investment as North Carolina does. One visible result of these changes is a dramatic growth in the state's overall income. In 1980 North Carolina was forty-first out of the fifty states in average per-person income. In 1997, North Carolina's ranking in average per person income had shot up to thirty-first.

North Carolina's push for education does not come from a fear of what the future might bring. On the contrary the state is ready to embrace the future with open arms. The people of North Carolina are readying themselves for the challenges of the twenty-first century.

# Important Historical Events

**524**   Giovanni da Verrazano explores the coast of North Carolina.

**585**   Sir Walter Raleigh sends the first English settlers to North Carolina.

**587**   Sir Walter Raleigh sends another group of English settlers under the leadership of John White.

**629**   King Charles I gives the southern part of the English claim in Virginia to Sir Robert Heath.

**650**   Settlers establish the first permanent settlements in North Carolina.

**663**   King Charles II gives Carolina to eight nobles, called the Lords Proprietors.

**677**   The Culpeper Rebellion takes over the affairs of state.

**711**   The Tuscarora War begins.

**712**   The Carolina Colony is divided into North Carolina and South Carolina.

**713**   The settlers defeat the Tuscarora.

**729**   North Carolina becomes a royal colony.

**765**   The Sons of Liberty and the Regulators begin resisting British taxation.

**774**   Women meet at the Edenton Tea Party.

**776**   North Carolina delegates to the Continental Congress vote in favor of independence.

**789**   North Carolina becomes the twelfth state.

**835**   North Carolina revises its constitution to allow its western part more power.

**861**   The Civil War begins, and North Carolina withdraws from the Union.

**868**   North Carolina rejoins the Union.

**1887**   The Farmers' Alliance is founded to help sharecroppers and small farmers form cooperatives.

**1903**   The first successful powered flight is made by Orville and Wilbur Wright, near Kitty Hawk.

**1911**   The United States Supreme Court divides the American Tobacco Company into four companies.

**1920**   North Carolina leads the country in all three of its major industries—tobacco, furniture, and textiles.

**1945**   Hydroelectric generators at Fontana Dam, the Tennessee Valley Authority's largest dam, provide electric power.

**1956**   The state General Assembly reacts to the Supreme Court's school desegregation ruling with proposed constitutional amendments.

**1960**   The first "lunch counter demonstration" is held in Greensboro.

**1963**   The University of North Carolina name is applied to state universities at Chapel Hill, Raleigh, and Greensboro.

**1971**   North Carolina adopts a new state constitution.

**1976**   A section of the historic New River is designated as a "scenic river" to keep a dam from being built on it.

**1988**   North Carolina suffers its worst drought and heat wave since the 1930s.

**1990**   The United States census reveals that North Carolina is the tenth most populated state in the Union.

**1994**   The North Carolina legislature imposes tougher penalties on adults who sell or give guns to children or teenagers.

The state flag consists of a blue stripe at the left, and one red and one white stripe across the remainder. On the blue stripe are the state's initials. Above and below the initials are dates on gold banners. The top date is the date Mecklenburg County declared its independence from Great Britain. The lower date is the date the state's delegates to the Continental Congress were instructed to vote for independence.

# North Carolina Almanac

**Nickname.** The Tar Heel State

**Capital.** Raleigh

**State Bird.** Cardinal

**State Mammal.** Gray squirrel

**State Flower.** Flowering dogwood

**State Tree.** Pine

**State Motto.** *Esse quam videri* (To be, rather than to seem)

**State Song.** "The Old North State"

**State Abbreviations.** N.C. (traditional); NC (postal)

**Statehood.** November 21, 1789, the 12th state

**Government.** Congress: U.S. senators, 2; U.S. representatives, 12. State Legislature: senators, 50; representatives, 120. Counties: 100

**Area.** 52,672 sq mi (136,421 sq km), 28th in size among the states

**Greatest Distances.** north/south, 188 mi (303 km); east/west, 499 mi (803 km). Coastline: 301 mi (484 km)

**Elevation.** Highest: Mount Mitchell, 6,684 ft (2,037 m). Lowest: sea level, along the coast

**Population.** 1990 Census: 6,657,630 (13% increase over 1980), 10th among the states. Density: 126 persons per sq mi (49 persons per sq km). Distribution: 50% rural, 50% urban. 1980 Census: 5,881,813

**Economy.** *Agriculture*: tobacco, broiler chickens, corn, soybeans, hogs, turkeys, cotton, peanuts, sweet potatoes, dairy products, apples, eggs, ducks. *Manufacturing*: textiles, tobacco products, chemical products, electrical equipment, machinery, food products, furniture. *Fishing*: flounder, crabs, oysters, croaker, shrimp, sea trout, clams. *Mining*: limestone, phosphate rock, sand and gravel

State Seal

State Flower:
Flowering dogwood

State Bird: Cardinal

# Annual Events

★ Pig Cookin' Contest in Newport (April)

★ Hang Gliding Spectacular in Nags Head (May)

★ National Hollerin' Contest in Spivey's Corner (June)

★ Summer Festival of Music in Brevard (June/August)

★ Craftsman's Fair in Asheville (August)

★ Mineral and Gem Festival in Spruce Pine (August)

★ Mountain Dance and Folk Festival in Asheville (August)

★ State Championship Horse Show in Raleigh (September)

★ National 500 Auto Race in Charlotte (October)

★ State Fair in Raleigh (October)

★ Anniversary of the First Powered Airplane in Flight in Kitty Hawk (December)

# Places to Visit

★ Bentonville Battlefield, near Smithfield

★ Biltmore Estate in Asheville

★ Blue Ridge Mountains, near Asheville

★ Cape Hatteras National Seashore, on the offshore islands

★ Cherokee Indian Reservation, at Cherokee

★ Chimney Rock in the Blue Ridge Mountains

★ Duke Homestead in Durham

★ Fort Raleigh National Historic Site, on Roanoke Island

★ Grandfather Mountain, near Linville

★ Great Smoky Mountains National Park, west of Asheville

★ Fort Bragg near Fayetteville

★ Morehead Planetarium in Chapel Hill

# Index